goddess gives sun enough

David C. McLean

POSTHUMAN POETRY & PROSE

First published in the world by POSTHUMAN POETRY & PROSE 2022

ISBN: 978-1-4717-2787-0

This is the first attempt at a book of poetry after the thirteen books in the "poems for Emma" series. It is the first book created entirely after McLean returned to the UK on the first of February, 2022

This book is dedicated to Linnet, who made all of this moving possible

Table of Contents

i. to begin

instead of archaic names

here were storms come, as winter dies to spring
the trees restored on hills passionate
as absence

we walk a memory encased in clay where ghosts go
feet & dreamer, here is mourning memory
heaven, here is sidewalk tiny

& time flies a kestrel in the untidy sky
where words are murderers there.
stones in the mud stand insistent

innocence. nothing is so empty, this plenum
a bramble madness. boots made for walking
or flesh to sweat in them:

a seagull assembles memory. he is heaven

here birds sing

here birds sing mourning song everything is; they dance as penny pigs memory was, & there is silence otherwise nighttime where all the ghosts are sleeping their insurrection, nowhere is everywhere is heaven potential

the birds sing us paleonymics invisible, they are madness one answer their defiant life, entropy is love or a cupboard potential, this is missing things innocence, this is living

the trees grow right down to ground, the flower is called Gary. night is not only nipples & madmen, it is arrogance spits defiance at time & night, it is monsters coming alive

smoke & innocence

i.

the leaves wait to cover the abstemious trees
like love does sunset, crawling through bodies
smoke & innocence, spring again
& all the pain gone missing
from the broken faces, memory
& dead men

once i burned for her time & fire, mourning
& a sword, memory tied us together broken bodies
in inexorable connection. flesh one heaven
together, one beast meaning scarred into us love
& everything blood to fuck enough
though centuries apart & damaged

i need goddess to roar from the ground like laughter
so i am tied to the night & this room grows solid
around me, as if i lived here, more than meat
defying entropy & cold stone, & the soil might open me
madness, absences might matter

ii.

yet goddess waits Her abyss indifferent,
fire for me memory, & nothing to happen again
my broken eye

i am alone & forever, dust & inglorious, cold glow
my compassionate ghost, spirits to brush me
one callous heart, blind my every eye

not a finger

it is not a finger or an index,
not any significant indexical
the trace running this,
want to say & *maybe*

i do not know
what the ghost expects;
memory & madness,
whatever

passion screamed skin once
cozy suffering, blood to live in
flesh & nothing, lies & nighttime

but this does not point *beyond*
or anywhere important,
& every finger is distant
forever

only the ghost listens
where words were;
she is always here -

i don't know how to burn

here is every always

here is every always inside, around me one nighttime one daylight life, goddess storm the star carpet She sings us every absence, She screams in me Her madness, archaic & Africa, butterflies & mitochondrial Eve where words are burning here & time is not for dreaming in, here is everything & oblivion

what stops is nipples is not; memory or everything forgotten, the trace is the ghost in us love, the decay of some prurient Platonism intensity & fire alive the skin, home & ghost psychosis, here is insincere & left us every nowhere

indigo

here is the bruise obscene,
the eye memory expectant;

we do not recognize ghosts
always, they sleep standing

answers. the music one string
invisible, the night is color

love, blood, & brutal us;
one vicious innocence, indigo

sing us flesh & intense,
blue is a bruise

flowers fall

flowers fall their suicide
as the penny pigs dream vengeance
heaven under them

nighttime alive one chocolate teapot
where nothing gushes love
above us

listen, the songbird sings innocence,
though there is crisis here so flowers fall
& i need headphones better

because flowers fall forever,
& there are too few ghosts,
blood & hopeless,

& everything resurrected
for these dead things singing,
only the penny pigs are living

one several remedy

this is forever was, love us
one several remedy, maybe,

snow & laborious homewards.
goddess remembers the ghost goes;

she sits still beside me & nothing matters,
not every absence

& here television erected
one sumptuous structure,

world & everything there;
goddess dropped words in me

& ghost to keep me safely.
it blazes here beast intensity

fire forever, under us is earth
& meat loves to fuck & burn;

there is no such thing as world
here, no real words

the ghost is muscle love

the ghost is holy, she is muscle love;
i do not know what invented her

she defers to nothing, not even me
beast or the tiniest animal ever

with every squalid expectation
rooting in the fucking shrubbery

drinking blood enough. ghost was always
here beside me recapitulating memory

goddess was, she indicated Her
trust us, one insignificant gesture

forever. effervescent was
& every god forgotten, history turns here

& we return here to burn, all the rest
one sad machinery stopping:

goddess inside us fire alive
& everything else forgotten

one may listen

i do not know one may listen
beyond ghost,

& maybe other dead children, living
insistence a tensor in unrepentant flesh;

every intensity trembling unto death
sex was, nipple is innocent -

i am twisted. here world glows
insatiable faceless;

there is one may listen once
maybe, goddess remains;

the rest fades away

here is sunrise

here is sunrise explodes in me
one adequate resurrection;

the church stands godless & moss,
penny sows that plow their memory

through grass dancing over damp soil
alive, a more adequate carpet for them.

it is anxiety they eat, it is dreams
being me; so love us once heroin sunset

again, but it is sunrise here & explicit
woodlice: soil is moist touch, memory

enough is enough

names i never knew

here i wear all the names i never knew, innocent
paleonymics, & all the ghosts homeless in me
memory

here It lives resurrected again, nonsensical
recollected, everything that never happened
madness & happiness

goddess has dressed us this heritage in skin
& hopeless bone: sexless flesh where ghosts go,
though nothing dies alone

sun comes an interloper

sun comes, an interloper dressed in cloud sky above all this idiot history, the defective ramble, all their bruised words are just cum dribbling from a dead ass, to assemble some scumbag heaven for them; they are boneless epigones, less than all the honest dead men

i breathe me some scumbag summer, & the earth lies loveless nothing under us, i am dead flesh & every expectancy disassembled here, nothing to touch me & nothing coming, this meat to bleed easy its futility, nothing left to believe or be, & only this one little ghost left to love me

words were always damage madness & sad as syntax, but goddess is all i ever needed to be free

in the dirt

in the dirt flowers are summering bloom
& tired of waiting patient like the trees do,

tress who carry their sap heavy under soil
where dying animals come home

to feed them meat, meaning, love
forever. the tress wait their winter

defiant life. in the dirt is beast being,
return eternal heaven this dead flesh

where everything is love goddess gives,
is summer snowflakes of time alive

teapot is empty a memory

teapot is empty a memory a flesh sexual; it burns meat here, meaning & to be.

forever is assembled once i have forgotten it, it seemed passion one absence, & every death in me was resurrected again, a sufficient connection

all there is remains one ghost, ghastly this madness was, everything else inconsequential. empty is teapot dream, all the importunate flesh, for here is sex & empty forever - animals sing winter sun coming, so love them goddess, love them Her forever

i do not see anything else matters, madness & happenstance, & i am nowhere beast to be, thus freedom my only meat being me

it is real things, images evanescent

it is real things, images evanescent
for fire is goddess flesh in Her
where earth lives blood
& recurrent

it is a ghost an open insurrection
& love is a flower, a fire,
it is always elsewhere

here is absence solidified

here is absence solidified gray & maybe
because ghosts are chalk on a blackboard
& the uniform is unnatural fiber,
a ghastly answer

the faces are crumpled anxiety,
i wore them like memory was
recurrent nothing

there are ancestors dressed in blood,
drums, & absolution;
the goddess recollects them
a scream & a meaning

in me this lack is everything missing -
words their shoddy suicide
& a ghost floating through vacuum,
meat & perfectly free

the cage is angry

the cage is angry one memory
budgerigar recurrent

& death a grotesque interloper
shabby nipple scissors

i run over sand madness
hoping a broken bottle

a ghost to go home

whatever goddess said

whatever goddess said i admit it seems like gibberish;
i do not understand Her ancient language
or any name She says *memory*

She laughs Her anger Her holy psychosis
& every ghost is homeless,
until She pulls us home into Her fire

meat screaming its intensity resurrection,
its sex incessant. whatever goddess said;
i listen always She screams night

& the ghost waits her patient,
watching me flesh & heaven
because every word here is a prayer

& burns. She likes it to hurt
some savage love. She is love.
good for Her

the sky one fire

we are stardust, the ancient cliché tells us,
but so is feces & garbage;
stardust are all the scum

& yet the sky is always one fire
because it is goddess everywhere
the love & fire inside Her

& they will fall forgotten their blind
shallow eye, but goddess
Her wild fire -

i burn forever there

here once monsters

here once monsters, time & eyes they spatter resurrection seminal, ghosts they come fangs & absence, night the divine rat's asshole strapped to untidy sky alight

there is no insurrection inevitable, the shoddy sidewalk the nighttime inside them empty & insufferable. pigeons work their gormless, they are made of paper explosion, they only come in rough numbers like love does

seagull, sing me oblivion, come let us sing heroin sunset, death or savage sex, sing us insatiable nipple next

way too much human

here history lives; they say it smells like idiot scissors, the medical certitude beyond sex & reflection, & death a snug cupboard forever where corpses snuggle nothing

they swarm here, vermin walking their obnoxious incessant, some humanist madness renascent & nothing worth recollecting forever, goddess has forgotten already. she screams her meaning in me, the beast walks patient its passion, its sexual psychosis inside me meat, nothing under the sun to touch enough, & their haggard human void hangs gray its empty

here is beast blood intensity fucking orgasm in me, not everything that is deserves to return, so She tells me - there is too little beast, way too much human, too little being

this is not real

this is not real, it is invisible
this; here i am missing, this lack
my absence, tattered paper memory
was & no love under the sun
much, nothing inside me
lifeline, nothing to touch

goddess shows

goddess shows this is corpse once;
She is hunched & laughing Her madness

screams at me instead of memory
i have rejected, this is Her cave

faceless where everything burns
into smoke & words. meat dreams

memory, & spirit itself is flesh
unfolding blood-flower, scream

& being, here is Cadaver i am
resurrected in Her forever;

sex & nothing heaven

Cadaver forgets

Cadaver waits his insolent heaven,
flesh & forgetful

here is Earth under him he knows
answer lives there concealed

beast meaning; it is goddess
presents him sunrise once,

night in him a scar, an abnegation,
manic Cadaver is waiting

here the dead were

there is only this massive history, ancestors
howling one psychosis, rage under black sky
mourning their flesh forgotten

warriors who carried axes to civilized walls
& borders, here the dead were once
one savage meat burning their intensity

together, fang & a madness, goddess Her idol
looming in the wildness nighttime,
& memory made of damage absences,

the cryptic glyphs written in children
scars on the thinnest skin, nightmare
scribbled in them, dead men already

& yet dead ancestors wait for us
blood & skull, savage inside me
memory, & nothing left to touch or love

the soil clings

the soil clings to my boots like protection, like love from earth under us, footsteps this bruised nothing & the sky a gray cage over us & sun to touch it like a drug, like innocent fingers, & summer hides behind the sky an angry savage fuck

the soil clings to my boots like a bug does, tiny & far too much

the trees slow summering

trees dance their slow summering
static absence, buds a brutal eye
nighttime, sing me immobility

a tiny mouse, an ashtray heart,
& woodlice to dance me madness
where world is slow to start

this is remembered

this is remembered, memory
dissembled

& put back together one image
slow & sunrise

grass i have forgotten
as were it ephemeral

every god forgotten.
& goddess hides

in flowers where love does
Her shady psychosis -

all the ghosts walk with us
to leave night homeless

one dead soldier

acephalic sunset

once comes acephalic sunset then spider
nighttime, the dead remember us, body
without organs of speech or vision
living

there is no resurrection yet, arbitrary answer
this exploding hopeless inevitable,
daydream & maybe. she said
expectant -

paint me meaning blood one sky on fire
please, here is memory
forgot to be

the skin shivers

in the skin trembles flesh expectant, passion
one intensity, fire alight & sparks
to answer shiver skin

& words to assemble us memory, identity
dressed in sexed meat meanings written
their palimpsest scars & madness,

nipples interstitial, & beast being trickling
seed into corners wrapped around rooms
where nothing lives its impatient wait

eternity. the skin shivers scars its innocence
& ample absence, intense in the burning skin
one love cadaver lives

intense is a color

intense is a color, passion fire
burning indigo heart

some sumptuous eternity;
a tree in flames,

an ancient garden
where ghosts sleep summer

sunlight, intense a color
a word to burn,

a world

sunset swells storm & mourning

sunset swells storm & mourning the shortest eternity, summer hangs sugar & flowers on fire, waiting in the wings to strut the scene its intemperate ejaculation

there is time & everything on fire, memory an ash, an absence, ashtray madness here are all the gods forgotten, nipples & everything unforgivable, heaven the resident erection, storm & mourning come to sing us structure & sunset - pressure drop better than the rest, pressure drop & forget everything else

here is wood & greening

here is wood & greening staggers drunk
over the moist soil,
open to us like an expectation,
a savage answer

maybe it is waiting to hold a tiny flower
goddess gives, i might touch Her color
adorning it, like a priest
carries heaven in his hands to an altar,
an impossible blessing

here is wood & water to empty into it
memory, everything the flesh has forgotten
once, the wood is screaming meaning,
the city mumbles in its sleep,
only goddess gives being & to be

there is blood under it

there is blood under it, this skin stretched over the patient night awaiting its explosion, wild sidewalk ecstasy pulling intensity over me, its tattered red banners to wrap me passion

this is the liminal, the intensity we read after it has been a scar in us, already written its savage glory, the love that flutters past, effulgent, to make us the madness we are

there are bodies for spirit, this tiny instant, alive to grow them resurrection, flesh & blood touch us nothing, goddess Her warriors, to grow us whole one eternal second, wrapped in red passion, wrapped in words, wrapped in sex & flesh & heaven

here Cadaver quickens

here Cadaver quickens in me,
a beating root growing through dry bone
wrapped in scars & melancholia,
this palimpsest skin i writ me in,
every memory assembled
to sing like dead men laughing

for fingers need to touch, & forever everywhere
the scream sings at the heart of the meat,
the slow statue love grows deathless in the flesh
erect, or spanked intimate as madness
across the savage lap

goddess carries us dust in the wind
this implausible story She has scribbled in us
Her firefly nighttime

passion comes the tiniest dancer;
Cadaver stirs as he hears her sing

gray & disintegrate

i.

day grows gray & disintegrate, eternal vermin i am, & disconsolate heaven burning here star in me, dust & sunset memory; this is walking sullen sidewalk every incommensurable intensity, what burns is this tingle the skin; it is excited & love is not a number

i do not even know if the total number of pigeons is odd or even, i know summer stardust touch us flesh, & it is spirit that establishes connections, it is sketches of every plausible reincarnation goddess might grant us once, skin is a shiver & loves to touch

ii.

day marches an army carrying flags & banners through the tattered tapestry scars i am, sex & flesh & resurrection potential

iii.

the ghosts stagger in me madness, stardust heartache in me, broken girl, she is still living in me our sexual memory, here is where words go home once, run to you one manic melancholy, ashes to burn world, it is wet fire here, touch & punish us, for where i live is goddess given, she calls this Her earth

this room is on fire for you always, everything here burns

kiss & sunshine

she walks into me a kiss & sunshine
so old melancholia falls fragment
& shatter, peeling me scars absent,
this intensity shiver me oblivion
skin

she would fit under an arm she tells me,
like memory a thousand lifetimes
forever this very second

she walks through my ghost a kiss
& a lifeline, so words burn into me
a sleeping tattoo

come, breathe me meaning a dream
flesh & heaven, writhe me my fire;
i burn easy, like a wooden spoon

& nothing here is really true

several comes summer

several comes summer, expectant
flesh & memory to collect

dead leaves on a sleeping tree, earth
under us, rooted in love or mud

& nothing better than earth here
where goddess marches Her animal

arc between us, nothing more real
than nobility you painted me, eyes

alive, a heart full of burning time,
& hearts where madness dances

she paints memory assembled together

she paints earth goddess gave us, spirit & living things, earth they aspire to fold like a ghost under this foolish world where they assembled madness their grotesque ambition, ashtrays & military precision

she paints me the broken bone of love, some shoddy glory, carried an eye, a madness, a night alive, heroin & razor-wire lifeline

strapped to the canvas blood & the sun, the dismembering that remembers itself there, she paints what is real hidden inside their broken human world

the cat jumps

the cat jumps on the bed
feral memory

he is not flesh & maybe never was,
spirit & not a real ghost,

like the fox that watches
anxious & flowers.

at dawn i heard the songbird
who visits her first nest now

& is missing from this place
where poetry lives,

where she roars her agnostic mourning,
death & festive flesh;

she spoke of a lady that invited her
somewhere, then denied something;

i almost asked aloud what she meant
before i remembered that ghosts of flesh

leave pools of spirit, like bloodstains
scattered behind them

if goddess blesses them
& they breathe being into art

wrapped in meat & dreams -
all the real ghosts were asleep

the dead grow silent

the dead grow silent now
their passionate wisdom concealed

except my every dead generation,
burning fury the voices they scream to me

in languages i cannot understand, roaring
like swords, these madmen,

screaming slaughter their sad dance,
emptying desire one intensity

into the silent night inside me,
to scream their dead psychosis free,

to sing me the meaning of my meat

the dead dance laughing

the dead dance laughing around me
drunk on their unicorn milk chocolate
teapot; this is woodlouse heaven
made of flesh & ghosts all full of dreams

sun screams broken flesh

when you have ghosts, you have everything
(Roky Ericksson)

i.

sun screams broken flesh & here trees stagger their impetuous spring, spitting green memory into the erased face winter was, defying entropy again like happy little madmen

the same scream sings in me this reassuring resurrection forever, the spell dispelled from the erect flesh, the magic words scribbled anxious their living into the shallow palimpsest skin, where melancholy history sits, a pitcher of innocence that listens

ii.

goddess has sometimes given me memory, the ass of madness to spank, timeless a long cold night & love never listens, it drinks unicorn milk & sings us oblivious, night an empty ashtray & faces swarm there insane, rising through the water they are life & a nightmare, the invisible cat stares at my ghost, she is always patient & ignores him, for words have become our only home

iii.

sun screams broken flesh, a dog howling eternal return, beer & murder here

night has ended & fallen into mourning, there is dance in me one ghost psychosis, flesh intensity the scream the goddess dropped into the meat

because once love was stardust & art was more than meaning was, more than syntax or seedy sememes, scribbling nipples & shabby semantics

iv.

here is shatter absence, here is recollection & return forever, love & flesh like goddess tells us here i sit & burning; this is ghosts & earth where everything returns - it is forever & i am this insistence - i am always burning here

the willows

the trees tremble erect their passion
defiant life

they scream one green meaning
under desirous skies

alive. you show me summer
comes a sleepy resurrection

& trees their song of tomorrow
give blood to us, their sap

singing sublime madness, words
& home slumbering sunshine

ii.

the trees dream here
their ancient memory;

the ghosts are sleeping now
& we are their eyes

here heaven sings

here heaven sings a silent flat,
the sun opening windows with light
alive. flowers stretch incandescent
their naked truth, sexual insurrection
their seed of meaning given me

& goddess humming within everything
living; she is life wild, & the fire defiant
falling bravely into death erect,
the love that holds ghosts whole.

& outside foxes watch, flicker into existence
like flame wrapped around night
to hold me in this cold inside

the meat that thinks & loves & lives
burning here forever already,
heaven flesh that goddess gives,
words & things

this goddess has given

i see this goddess has given us Her innocence;
the trees that strain their love to touch sun
erect, life returning into generous mulch

the nameless decay of tiny animals crawling life
fire, to die them back to brutal roots, to be food
their passionate fruition, forgotten flesh

falling to the fang of absence. happy mania
goddess has given me, words one history
dusty as love. the trees strain life here,

& flesh is forever to touch like the sun
above, everything goddess has given us,
bone & skin & stardust

clouds & sun standing

the sun stands a soldier waiting his patience, he is light sky clouds dancing them their madness; happy is arrogance is starlight

light smells like forever & the narcissi in the bowl are racing their savage victory, green meaning them a promise of return, like memory was; life is a scream insistent in the meat, in the flesh of plants & beasts, their sad passionate

there is absence here, there is night everywhere, but there are clouds under the goddess, under the sun, where goddess is lives meat & love; there is always Her fire thundering in the brutal blood

wet soil

the rich wet soil is goddess touching Her earth
to bless me mud & memory forever; dirt here

is full of death, recycled life & timeless
flesh today resurrected in me,

meat for the feeding. these trees stagger love
under cobbled clouds their morning

dissemination, they stretch heaven inside them
the throbbing sap rising erect salvation

to wash winter away, they spit leaves dreamless
into winter's wrinkled face, there are ghosts here,

beasts & passionate, spirits of place

mud covers me

mud covers me
like memory covers love

once, flesh & sex
becoming death

& insolent resurrection
again

here is wood & mourning
dissipated - smoke

& bones, sun
& hope

let this not be sunset yet

dawn falls over this land a weight
expectant, spring in it a flower
coming later, the trees bowed
their tolerant desire, ancient
patience, & leaves burst flame
their passion a noisy life

maybe they sing back to songbird
words she has given them, maybe
they are more than budding nothing
& trees hold more meaning
than these people without dreams,
sleepwalking their memory empty?

i shall sing the scream of these trees
as goddess permits me, fire
& a scream to comfort them
their insolent winter, let this not
be sunset yet, let branches stretch
their incessant regeneration

& the tiniest mouse remember them

it is life always

under the soil is life always burgeoning its wait, now flowers spring happy as the terrible return of the many dead that have surrendered themselves to ash & madness, all these gone generations remembering themselves their dismembering, fresh flesh their blooming fruit; & every branch & every animal is goddess thrusting forth Her abundant love, Her earth that shelters everything & shelters us

tears dry with time, but there are always trees shouting night's defiance under goddess' sky. & this shall survive - for everywhere is the throb of this passionate savage madness, the seed that swarms is always alive

carpet full of savage stars

the carpet is full of savage stars,
tiny memory

under one insolent television
to spell us ideology

forgotten. thus is water
a hopeful ocean;

the woodlice assemble them
dead again

& love is a spotless kitchen
where ghosts sleep

full of silent dreams
& nothing is screaming,

a carpet full of savage stars
where the ghosts are sleeping

manic cornucopia

it is blood the memory, telegraph
& sexless lexis

everything is forgotten the flesh was
manic cornucopia -

nighttime swallows the gormless gods
& all the ghosts are homeless

seeds like a hammer

the sun throws the trees into me a hammer;
zopyra are sparks their eternal life,
thrown out of me words internal
& goddess burning there,
meaning this semen swarming

light. here is shatter inside glow me
memory; it is not always night

statue in the stone

the statue sleeps manic in the marble
& words are disposition exquisite
goddess said in me blood & cum
nothing

light is a knife made of time & sex
memory, here is extended the faint
history one squalid resurrection -
& everywhere humanity, shit
& idiots

the statue sleeps in the stone
its crippled love

light is a knife & time
is nothing to touch

sense certainty probably

all i need is sense certainty probably, not specific perception the sexual flesh - just goddess looming Her fire in everything is living & flame dashing sparks out of this the meat me, hammer & manic anvil where meaning breathes memory together vague figures struggle like force & understanding, their massive shadows dancing over the ghost face identity, caverns & madness

It throbs one roar in my veins, the sap of a million trees this passion resolved into conflagration, razor stripes & time, here is the nerve, the sex, the sweating flesh, night is alive & everything else is lies their asinine, one weak human emptiness inside - only the beast is meaning & the beast is always mine

earth answers archaic

no images & no distinctions drawn
there is an intensity left beyond representation,

it is static madness hangs in coils of time,
memory made of meat & alive

& all of earth a solemn sheltering
that the one goddess has given,

present & the every presencing,
a box full of ghosts & their seed sparks

where nothing is absent, nothing
is lacking;

it burns one eternity
this still instant,

flesh & forgiven,
earth to answer us

& nothing to love:
this is enough

pragmata entwined in discourse

i.

i saw once *pragmata* entwined in discourse that is silent again here, preserved a power coiled in the flesh so prayer is opened, petals into the hands of goddess Her savage answer, i sing Her this one scream i repeat forever because prayer & devotion is madness, is the only praxis that matters

words fall their silent spiral into unmeaning, stripped flesh from the sad semantic i shall burn them world here

ii.

there are ancient names left me i burn for Her, goddess Her memory me, skin & oblivion

it gives the incessant flesh, the shiver that thunders inside the skin & cannot be weighed or written, the priceless meaning that insists on oblivion

iii.

this is bone where ghosts go, recollected their dismembering remembered, preserved one holy psychosis screaming in the meaning meat, one flame forever & a coffin full of dreams

blackbird stands its madness

blackbird stands its madness, perched
singing oblivion its vocal tree

an old man, angry at god, screaming on a hill
& nothing listens to him

his fire roaring there incessant ember,
red flesh he resurrects him

the blackbird stands its madness
& does not need to be forgiven

or to reason or mean anything
beyond the brute persistence of being

songbird does not know

the songbird does not know her words burn
better, ash & madness a million wings
innocent

stretched across the sky nighttime living
pinions, memory is made of blood
& earth swells precious its flesh

goddess has given. there are words
one seed burning everywhere, songbird
knows where they are hidden,

she burns their meaning into them

the hammer that values

here is spark & ash, the seeds that are beaten
meaning, the hammer that values,
that destroys what does not earn its being;

it is night already everywhere
& night is desire is bleeding

birds sing invisible

birds sing invisible their broken night,
shatter fragment

for nothing is damage like a songbird
silent, furious her fire;

so i weep for what is lacking her,
wings an innocence,

madness the caverns, the ghosts scream
me one more meaning

where songbird sings silent
& nothing is forgiven

ii. to extend

this is grounded

this is grounded where earth lies its anguish,
sheltering

memory a barbarian shell screams *return us
love, flesh & effervescent*

sex. the goddess makes trees a forest
arches one madness

panic stalks the shadow suburb
nothing rests above it

the mania, the mind, the melancholy
they touch enough

here is always

here is always the archaic answer,
meat meaning in the goddess
where trees stretch their defiant answer,
sky a nighttime alive

& ice a subtle structure
where words preserve their deft intent
curled in songbird fingers, wings
& everything missing, madness
or the saddest lack

there is time inside the living flesh
forever, & some words still know to burn
the roar of the tiniest animal
singing her ghost psychosis
& every night feathers on fire
alive; there are words still left
that point towards earth

the ghosts one feather flesh

the ghosts sing them together feather flesh
these irreducible fragments

innocence listen us walk a corpse
& here is meaning imbricated,

dense shadows holding together
sex & reflection

there are words eternity
goddess has given to sing

one tiny loving skull
full of everything

instead of recollection

instead of reflection recollected
i assemble me flesh fire
together, the fury of ghosts
thunder us one blood

& the seagulls sing us forgiveness
their shabby slaughter; soil is numb
meat that keeps one dream life
alive & timeless, insolent

a nipple. here is hidden earth
just under these surfaces, world
& goddess gives us everywhere.
She does not forget to burn

it sings rainlight

it sings rainlight under sky
the wet that ties us love under goddess
its ineluctable touch

this gray day the trees grow madness
my salvation in me, palimpsest
this illegible memory

the wait of the day safe as a tiny mouse
hidden from this cotton-candy Armageddon
better than all the dead

waiting to fly & rise & roar an insensible
Phoenix resurrection, burning
& words. until then it gives

rainlight, this gray that burns here

it gives this earth here

i.

it gives this earth here, night & a sky timeless, earth it is Her granting
where She shelters every fragment goddess has left scattered madness,
bodies meaning flesh & resurrection forever, memory & dead men,
paws the savage answer

ii.

it is wet this pavement subservient to sky washing dreams asleep. the
land arches its bowed sullen love: awareness is meat mostly, sex &
inattention; resolute is heaven

earth answers archaic (ii)

i.

earth answers archaic, goddess
Her voice, sing in me memory
the dead beasts have crawled
flesh returns soil & forgiveness, given
them innocent & sex forever, madness
the answer

burn here world is, idiot meat
meaning & *nothing needs forgiving*
She said forever

ii.

& the self is poison Artaud said it was, a ghost screaming angry his
nothing in a box they assume to be full of god, full of everything else
ego & forgotten. absences do not matter; they are defects of attention,
for all there is that is real is burn fire eternity, goddess forever one
intensity. it is this depth & sex an instant forever, *nunc stans* madness
fuck happenstance - here is soil & trees seed one return, one purpose
burning for Her

iii.

i forget this, world the medium idiot fish glimpse it dreams of being;
earth answers archaic they do not know to listen, & it echoes
significance; nothing means but passion, it is one screaming

sleepy epistemic

they dream them this sleepy epistemic,
apples & oranges

& all the gods forgotten,
but the arrogance that dwells in them,

shallow self-appointed madmen
manqués. they do not think

unforgivable, they do not live
in their pointless world

so far from earth,. & goddess
does not worry about this -

for it is here we are burning
eternal; they shall never return

it is fire teardrop

it is fire teardrop, gods absconding
& all that bellows memory was
the tiniest mouse, sparks
& one madness

there are woods to walk, lacking wolves
or even axes, feet happy the intractable
grass, burning here water
returning eternity, drops

for goddess, world well forgotten,
for what falls shall rise again
Her fire; She gives you this
innocent, earth as it lives

winter breaks

i.

winter breaks ice flower this tangible dispersal, psychotic diaspora all the intensity the sun swallowed & every god that never was reflected in them, memory is for dead men

the ghosts walk cold & spring is upon us one ravening fang, sun one loveless, & the trees strain us their various reasons, hear & a madness i hear you scream skeleton roaring the vain wait, the futility scars over thin skin i have written me palimpsest invisible, like goddess skull everything fits into it every answer it carries illegible as names might be, this is the best of all possible murders & made of ghosts unmedicated, ghosts without diagnoses, ghosts hungry & hopeless, whereabouts unknown

ii.

summer sings dead memory & nipples to lick; the mouse is tiny though & strides like divinity over mountains & eternity: burdened by platitudes & inanity, carcass & madness, she screams an eagle draped her fire curtain: words are not things

iii.

i am ghost watching, & burning here is this return, another spring this perfect flesh insensate, here is earth, as many as necessary It gives, it burns words being is

the temerity of dead

godless this arrogant skin
meat to murder here

time folded into a box of apples
was

under rain one heaven is
forever; fire persists

& nothing to forgive

it is not heaven

it is not heaven expected, seed
& meaning, words on skin is the one book
She writes on things,

goddess does, it is meat in me
means memory, & theory
is all about love, fire

& stardust once, it is animals crawl
beast being me, & nothing comes
to touch us enough

heaven is sexual

they said heaven is sexual
insistent a nipple meaning, seed

or freedom, it is moving finger
written, it is heaven flesh

where nothing is missing, skin
that does not need forgiving

here is empty

here is empty & everything together, this plenum & perfect where nothing is distinction, & it is only perceptible where love is, where the goddess that is love is, one real earth under us, & nothing there except what burns & what deserves, nothing worth mentioning except what returns

there are differences, a ladder madness, goddess assumes distance & invisible so they do not see Her here; they do not know earth - you can see it is lacking in all their vacuous words

sun burdens soil

i.

sun burdens the soil its ecstasy; there is fire our shady paleonymics, a dusty structure infested with the ghosts that shudder through these curtains, like dead memory watering these fertile psychoses, dreams to be are scars & archaic, all the sexed palimpsest flesh - & *thunder is coming a swastika was*; a shoddy obligation, a box full of gods

& yet the burdened soil is dappled madness, & here meaning sleeps expectant, ready to enter us if we walk these woods & listen for the song of every dead animal surrendered to the roots to burn back to the sun like love does, the selfless surrender whereby they have given themselves, all these tiny dead, back to the wood in the trunk, like the *adiaphora* that is suffering, some perfect plenum full of cum & nothingness

ii.

here the tiny mouse rises to burn again, to burn her resurrection & prefigure ghosts coiled in the leaves forever like gobbets of meat & meaning, hammer & anvil madness & eternity under me is Goddess She dances manic

i like to think the hallway spider is running her rage through the streets a savage murder, i like to imagine she will return like an elective identity to sew being together again, to tie memories flesh together & help them end

the spider knows to sing the scream static that hangs here this mourning silence, the day is a shaded woodlouse carapace fallen into history, a glorious corpse. memory palimpsest eat me, my flesh goddess has given me gobbets

my thousand dead generations are fury in me always, the song of my people is not music, it is fire thunderous & the gibbering of broken ghosts, a knife in the eye of beauty

the scream is intensity it is where desire trembles into skin oblivion, ghosts & a scar, a tiny bubble of time inside

& the goddess has taught me to scream forever, scream meaning for this little ghost sitting on the quilt, the one who records each flickering flame, faithful as madness or a scar

iii.

there are ghosts & history, a recollected flesh made of my dismembering assembled again, nothing left me but to sing this scream forever until goddess asks me again & i assent to this, i tell Her there is nothing yet left me to affirm & the ghost & i ascend to burn in Her eternity, earth forever then one intensity sharp as jagged memory stronger than words, one flame to be & no more worlds

iv.

the sun shrouds us crucified childhood memory & monastic rectitude, *the burning one rises like truth*

the songbird sings silence best

the songbird sings silence best.
she carries sad & human always,

her strength a savage memory
& one dismal explosion, petals

burning trees like screams,
an inconceivable freedom;

the songbird sings a violin
so ghosts can bleed

the ghosts are assembled here flesh

the ghosts are assembled here flesh
one slow song forever, drum & love us
here the trees arise their portentous
lack, green a fever & shadows dance
madness, sing us skull & blood enough

some dreaded anniversary, future funerals
& mad Cadaver as he assembles himself
so goddess never forgets us, tomorrow
Her yesterday the bird that rises burning
to sing us some oblivion again

the ghosts are assembled here again flesh
they know; this their meet meat & home

the tiny mouse dances

the tiny mouse dances shadows
forgotten, she is made of words
& a sense of fitting time
alive, memory inexorable
all ears & eyes; it is never night
really, it is soon given her to fly

the kitten lives still

a kitten lives here spirit
invisible, it is patient a wait

dust & apparition, shadows
a cat to dance, perhaps.

so dream me these diseases,
kitten, let night collapse

iii. to disintegrate

goddess carries sun enough

goddess carries sun & trees
over sheltering earth, flags & fucking
banners, She carries words burning
madness answers in us, love

& blood, She sings Her scream louder
in the meat, She puts dreams here
in this cockroach heart, memory
in me is dust & one skull

goddess carries every single sun
& this i choose to call love, murder
enough, the trees stretch being
in the thin skin, drops of blood-flower

intensity, cum & touch

here the madness

here the madness answers us
singing the missing the skin
memory

all these in me, *membra
disiecta*, love us summer
a sunset

shadows dance

garbage

it burgeons this world, it is garbage
a box full of gods, egos dream their being
corpses walking

burn them their incessant word here
burn them again

return is not every body every soul
homeless

burn me one memory reflexive
extend in me

no ghosts are left me
nowhere is home

time one manic answer

it spells time one manic answer
chronology extended miscarried structure
of sentences - spell us this hopeless span

madness thus, nipples & paleonymics
a tail told by idiots: nothing listens
& nothing worth mentioning lives in it

despair travels fast, real is the lack,
& poems do not deign to exist, nothing
matters, there is nothing to forgive

all there is

all there is left me is goddess Her eye

fire; it is given to burn there, It gives

madness absent, ghost in me

every stupid expectation ever;

it disappears this every identity

yet It still burns here eternity

goddess Her flame here -

It gives earth

It gives Her

Lightning Source UK Ltd.
Milton Keynes UK
UKHW010738030522
402417UK00001B/220